CW00555192

RADICAL GAINS
THE GB PARK AND PIPE STORY

Glencoe Ski Centre, Scotland. 2011

FROM START TO SOCHI
A BRIEF HISTORY OF BRITISH FREE SKIING & SNOWBOARDING

THE ROOTS
BY PAT SHARPLES

In the early 1990s, snowboarding came along and kicked the shit out of skiing. Everyone under 25 was going straight into snowboarding and the ski industry had started to go pretty stale.

Back then, most hardcore British skiers like me were hitting the extreme and mogul competition circuit whilst living the full-on ski bum lifestyle: in the back of vans, cars, and cheap one-bedroom apartments where we would squeeze in eight people. It was all about doing anything we could to be on the mountain. While searching for work in Courchevel, I randomly spent a few weeks living in the ski lift pass office toilets! This situation eventually landed me a job with a chalet company, which provided me with food and board and, most importantly, a lift pass. I'd make beds, clean toilets, fix skis and serve breakfast in the mornings, then ski all afternoon and try and follow the dream of making it as a skier. All different aspects of skiing excited me, but hitting the bumps and constantly exploring the backcountry was the ultimate lifestyle.

My own story tells the tale of competitive British freeskiing at this time. I started competing on the Amateur European mogul tour and, in 1996, became European Amateur mogul champion. At one point, I gave the Olympic dream a shot myself by trying to qualify for moguls for the 1998 Olympics in Nagano, Japan. But without the aid of a team, coach or funding I certainly wasn't living the life of a well-grounded and committed athlete - far from it! I ended up blowing my ACL and meniscus in a Europa Cup event and that was pretty much the end of that dream.

Meanwhile, the wider ski industry was changing direction thanks to the inspiration of snowboarding. A huge development came when some of the top ski brands started making wider skis, which changed the way we could ski the backcountry and powder. In 1997, Salomon released the first ever twin tip ski (the Salomon 1080), which changed the game (and my life) forever.

Soon, videos emerged of the new Canadian 'Air Force' - a collection of top skiers including Mike Douglas, JF Cusson, JP Auclair and Vincent Dorian - skiing their new twin tips in the park (which back then were called snowboard parks), a development which allowed skiers to land and take off backwards and took the sport up another level overnight.

Jim Adlington. Franz Josef Glacier, New Zealand. 2000

Warren Smith. Backside of Mont Fort, Verbier, Switzerland. 2006

All this altered the way people looked at skiing. It was like a new sport was being created before our eyes, with new tricks literally being invented daily. It became a lifestyle, and was basically the beginning of the British freeski community. My sponsors Salomon sent me a pair of the new 1080 twin tips and, a little later, the Pocket Rockets, made for backcountry freestyle, and I began chasing new dreams and goals. Soon after, we began seeing British rippers make a name for themselves internationally as pro skiers. Jamie Strachan, who was based in Chamonix, led the charge in the backcountry as well as the park. Strachan was the first British skier to attract international sponsorship deals. He also helped brands with their ski designs, another breakthrough. Dave Young, nicknamed the Godfather of British freeskiing, was another key influence, pushing the progression of skiing in the park harder than anyone else. He's got the scars and injuries to prove it, too.

Other names followed: Tignes-based James Vernon, who competed on the Freeride World Tour and set up Freeride

Culture, the first dedicated UK freeski website. Next came Chris Fetcher, Glen Parsons and Jason Shutt, who were all making names for themselves and starring in the latest ski flicks and on the front covers of magazines.

Jim Adlington, founder of Planks, was another crucial figure. Jim was a fully-fledged ski bum back in the day, and was one of the first British skiers along with myself to be signed by Salomon. Like many of the UK's finest, Adlington grew up cutting the mustard on Dendix at his local ski slope, Kidsgrove, just a five-minute walk from his parents' house.

For over a decade, wearing gardening gloves and denim jeans and with support from his mentor and the owner of Kidsgrove, Chris Poole, Adlington dedicated his spare hours to skiing on plastic. And like future GB Park and Pipe stars James 'Woodsy' Woods, Katie Summerhayes, Jamie Nicholls and Billy Morgan, who all came from this dryslope scene, Jim went on to ski on the global circuit with the likes of Candide Thovex, Tanner Hall and Jon Olsson.

Murray Buchan. 360 tail grab. Saas Fee, Switzerland. 2007

Jamie Matthew. Cairngorm, Scotland. 2014

Perhaps more importantly, Jim's core attitude – "I ski because it makes me feel happy" – symbolized the appeal of this UK freeskiing outlook and helped lay the foundations of what was to come.

Warren Smith is another key figure in the story of UK freeskiing. His British Freeski camps and Verbier Ride events helped inspire a lot of kids to get into the sport. A number of them have gone on to become some of the biggest names in UK freeskiing, including Andy Bennett, Joe Tyler, Jamie Matthew, Eddie Thelwell, Jamie Cameron and even Paddy Graham, who has gone on to be one of the biggest freeski stars in the world. Around this time, with my own pro career winding down, I started focusing on coaching whenever I could. In the early 2000s, Warren Smith asked me to run his aforementioned British Freeski camps on the glacier in Tignes during the summer. These attracted passionate skiers of all abilities and ages, who sent it hard on and off the snow.

Everybody was experimenting with new tricks they'd seen their idols do in the movies. It wasn't about prepping for competitions; more about just sending it for the fun of it. I'm pretty sure on some camps we would have to take someone to hospital everyday. It was crazy, but always an incredible atmosphere.

The camps eventually moved to Saas Fee, which became the place to be every summer. It was here that the next generation of skiers started to attend, including some of the current GB Park and Pipe team, and the scene began to change and become more professional as the profile of the competitions improved.

Around this time, we set up the Salomon Grom camps, which saw us travel around the UK coaching and inspiring kids at their local ski centres. The buzz around these camps was insane, which in turn inspired ski centres across the land to invest in their own freestyle facilities. With these foundations in place, the UK scene began to explode. Dryslopes and indoor snow centres were rammed every week, with kids riding the jumps, rails and the specially designed parks. One of the centres that proved to be a particular breeding ground for progressive talent was the

Woodsy. Rodeo 540 high safety. Liberty Mountain Snowflex Centre, Lynchburg, Virginia, USA. 2009 11

Pat Sharples. Obergugl, Austria. 2008

Jason Shutt. Saas Fee glacier, Switzerland. 2003

Woodsy. Switch double rodeo 1080. Mottolino Snowpark, Italy. 2010

late Sheffield Ski Village. At the time, it was arguably the largest dry ski slope in Europe, providing year-round ski facilities for everybody from beginners to the new blood of freestyle shredders. This place had the only halfpipe in the UK, a selection of different jumps and rails and quarter pipes, as well as bumps and other creative features.

The AIM Series of events were another important development at this time, and was an explosion of progression across the UK. This was when the current crop of UK freeskiing names began to emerge, including a 14-year-old James 'Woodsy' Woods, Katie and Molly Summerhayes, Tyler Harding, Rowan Cheshire, Murray Buchan, Andy Matthew, James Machon, Joe Tomlinson, Pete Speight and many, many more. Looking back, the first thing that really clued me into Woodsy was his personality. We were at the British Championships in Laax and, despite never having taken part in a competition on snow before, he came and asked me for some advice. I'd just taken on the job as Salomon UK Freeski team manager and promptly made Woodsy my first ever signing!

Katie Summerhayes was another skier who stood out from the start, even at nine years old, when she came over to the Salomon Grom camps. Anything you taught her she would just pick up straight away. She was intimidating the boys twice her age. Rowan Cheshire was also only 9 or 10 when she came along to the Grom camps with her little brother and sister. She was fearless, always willing to take the big risks to push her progression.

Among many of our greats in GB Park and Pipe, Woodsy, Katie, Rowan and many more have paved the way for the younger generation. At Woodsy's first ever X Games appearance in 2011, he made the podium with a bronze medal. This was the first time I'd say the international freeski community knew there was a 100% legit superstar on the scene who had grown up learning on the dry slopes, and was a brilliant endorsement of the wider British freeskiing scene.

Pat Sharples is Head of Coaching for BSS

James Machon. Halfpipe night training. Rosa Khutor Extreme Park, Sochi 2014 Winter Olympic Games, Russia

Woodsy. Finished 5th at the men's freeski slopestyle final. Sochi 2014 Winter Olympic Games, Russia

Paddy Graham. Chamonix, France. 2011

Jo Howard. Riding fresh powder. Weardale Ski Club in the Pennines, England. 2010

LOOKING BACK
BY ED LEIGH

*"Snowboarding in Britain is like a bumblebee. It looks like
it shouldn't be able to fly, but for some reason it can"*

These are the words of Eddie Spearing, who along with a handful of other intrepid spirits back in the mid-1980s, laid the foundations for what British snowboarding is today.

They very neatly sum up the contradiction that has been woven into the very fabric of UK snowboarding culture since the beginning: that our little island nation, with no real mountains or Alpine culture to speak of, has always massively punched above its weight.

So how has UK snowboarding managed to transcend such unpromising beginnings and produce one of the world's most envied sliding sideways cultures? How exactly have our dryslopes, snowdomes and windswept Scottish resorts produced Jenny Jones, Billy Morgan, Katie Ormerod, Aimee Fuller and Jamie Nicholls, some of the most progressive and creative competitive snowboarders of the last decade?

After twenty years spent travelling to some of the biggest, most exclusive and remote snowboard events on the planet, I've got a few ideas. Sure, the classic British traits of humour and eccentricity have much to do with it. But I think it runs much deeper than that.

Personally, I think it's because it is impossible to foster an ego learning to snowboard in the UK. You can sell Milton Keynes anyway you want, but the fact is it is miles away, both spiritually and geographically, from the type of glitzy resorts our European peers learn to ride at. Similarly, riding in the UK itself takes passion and dedication. Our Highland resorts, lashed by winds and storms, do not give up their treasures easily.

One of the most enduring images I have of British snowboarding is from 2001. I was watching a couple of kids trade tricks in the rain-soaked depths of winter at Sheffield Ski Village. They were battered, drenched to the skin and having the time of their lives. Witness this scene, and I believe you can claim to have witnessed stoke in its purest form. So what are the roots of this windswept, bloody-minded obsession with snowboarding?

The first snowboard landed in the UK with Hew Parsons, the owner of Outdoor Action in Cardiff, in 1984. Over the ensuing five years, the scene continued to grow rapidly; so much so that by 1989, the British Snowboard Association was formally established.

Hamish McKnight. Freeriding in Shemshak, Iran. 2005

Nelson Pratt. Riding the tree line. Gulmarg, Kashmir, India. 2007

Jamie Nicholls. AIM Series. High Wycombe, England. 2002

James Carr. Milton Keynes Snozone, England. 2009

Danny Wheeler. Ski Rossendale, England. Circa 1991/2

Danny Wheeler. Switch BS 900. Mayrhofen, Austria. 2007

As a nationally recognised governing body, the BSA had the authority to sanction the inaugural British Snowboard Championships in Aviemore, Scotland. 30 years later, 'the Brits' is still going strong and remains the on-snow hub for the entire British scene, providing a platform that enables our emerging talent to get to grips with real snow and learn the ropes of elite competition.

More importantly, it is an event that sums up the inclusiveness of the British scene. One of my favourite aspects of the 2018 Brits was seeing elite level riders like Billy Morgan, Jamie Nicholls and Aimee Fuller in attendance. They came to wind down after Korea and offered our rising stars the chance to pit themselves against the best to see how they measure up.

The establishment of the BSA was followed in 1991 by the first issue of Snowboard UK magazine. Helmed by Eddie Spearing and Mark 'Stig' Sturgeon, SUK was crucial to the development of snowboarding in Britain.

With Eddie at the wheel, this passionate, mischievous magazine epitomised the spirit of UK snowboarding. It spawned healthy competition in later magazines like Snowboard World, Whitelines and Document, and ultimately laid the foundations for the nascent British industry.

Working in tandem, the BSA and SUK helped connect the individual pockets of snowboarding that had sprung up around the country into one cohesive whole. Early pioneers

James Stentiford. Alaska. 2004

Lesley McKenna. FS indy. Halfpipe training at the Turin 2006 Olympic Winter Games, Italy

Jenny Jones. Kommunity Summercamp. Les Deux Alpes, France. 1998

Dan Wakeham. Frontside air. Avoriaz skatepark, France. 2009

Dan Wakeham and Dom Harrington. Les Deux Alpes, France. 2008

included Al Flemming and Gus Gillard of Acid Snow (an early British snowboard brand which appears even more outrageously ahead of its time with every passing year); and peers such as Rob Needham, Jeremy Sladen, Steve Crampton, Chod Thomas, Ian Cocking, Mark Webster, Simon Smith, Phil Young, Tony Brown and Dean Stoppani.

Their passion inspired the next generation, names like James Stentiford, Chris Moran, Stuart Brass, Steve Bailey and Justin Allison. These were the first British snowboarders to gain international prominence, their talent measuring up to the world's best and receiving the ultimate accolade of being featured in the pages of Transworld, snowboarding's bible at the time.

In 1994 I remember smuggling a huge inferiority complex over the Channel to France for my first season. I was a sponsored British snowboarder and having only ridden real snow a handful of times I was sure the mercurial French riders would laugh or pour scorn on me (they didn't; they were fascinated). But I drew huge strength, pride and belief from Chris, Stenti, Justin, Stu and Steve's accomplishments. They had paved the way for British snowboarders to be taken seriously, and showed the next generation what was possible.

At the same time, the domestic scene continued to thrive, with events like the Covent Garden Big Air and Board X bringing the world's best riders to our shores; and the Annual British Dryslope Championships (a full-blown riot at Sheffield complete with caravan rolling down the hill

anyone?), SUK and Whitelines giving everyone a real sense of belonging.

By the mid-to-late 90s, a new generation of even more impressive riders such as Simon Brass, Gary Greenshields and Scott McMorris were about to make their mark. They were led by a rider who spanned three generations of British snowboarding and was the visionary rider the UK needed at just the right time: Danny Wheeler.

Prodigiously talented, Danny measured himself against the best in the world and, at a time when most snowboarders were content to squander a good chunk of their talent partying, had the attitude to back up the ambition. He epitomised dedication and style, a formidable combination that helped drag UK freestyle into the 21st century.

While Danny blazed his trail, Melanie Leando and Lesley McKenna were striking out on a radically different but equally important path, following the example set by competitive UK pioneers such as Neil McNab, Becci Malthouse, Lloyd Rogers and Lisa Fletcher. Snowboarding was now part of the Olympics, and the two friends made a pact to try and get there.

They worked tirelessly together, supporting each other as they self-funded seasons chasing the world tour. In the end only Lesley made it. In 2002, she became Britain's first snowboarding Olympian, going on to compete at the Turin Olympics in 2006 and Vancouver in 2010. With no official UK Sport support for snowboarding at this time, her 17th in

Ben Kilner. Frontside air. Copper Mountain, Colorado. USA. 2012

Dom Harrington. Olympic test event. Sochi, Russia. 2013

2002 was an outstanding achievement. Lesley's World Cup and Olympic experience would also be vital in laying the foundations of what was to come. Her 15-year competitive career and her desire to use that experience to underpin the current GB Park and Pipe team has been a key factor in driving British success at the highest level.

Another key development in UK snowboarding was also unfolding at this time thanks to two teenage groms from Tamworth: Tim Warwood and Adam Gendle. This was the video part era, when every rider aspired to appear in films by Whitey, Mack Dawg and Absinthe. Unfortunately, a part in these films could cost anywhere between $20k and $40k, a level of industry support unheard of for a British snowboarder.

Step forward the universally-loved 'Tim & Gendle', who bridged this gap with a series of films that documented British snowboarding in all its unique, idiosyncratic glory.

Tim and Gend's passion, work ethic and sense of humour allowed them to turn what international critics would call average filming and riding into very entertaining films. Not everybody understood their inclusive approach, but this open attitude, combined with the fact that they never took themselves or snowboarding too seriously, set the tone for British snowboarding going into the 21st century.

Go back and watch Tim and Gendle's oeuvre today and one things stands out: the meteoric rise of Jenny Jones.

Between 2003 and 2011, Jenny pushed herself relentlessly, demonstrating an appetite for progression that would see her step onto the world stage with her first big win at the Honda Session in Vail. By 2008, she was at her peak, winning three X Games gold medals and dominating women's snowboarding during a three-year purple patch that saw her take the most technical tricks to the biggest kickers, at a time when few women were ready to step up

Billy Morgan. Wins big air at the Brits. Laax, Switzerland. 2010

Jenny Jones. The women's snowboard slopestyle final at the Sochi 2014 Olympic Winter Games, Russia

Jamie Nicholls. Finished 6th at the men's snowboard slopestyle
final. Sochi 2014 Winter Olympic Games, Russia

to the men's kickers on slopestyle courses. Had slopestyle been included at Vancouver in 2010, gold would have been all but a formality for Jenny.

Instead, it would be another four years before Jenny could make her mark at the Olympics, at the inaugural slopestyle event at Sochi in 2014. 30 winters after the first snowboard arrived in Britain, Jenny beat a new generation of emerging international talent to take bronze.

I've commentated on six Olympic Games and have seen a lot of Brits win medals during that time. But none of them have connected like that. Knowing how deep the ties run in British snowboarding, and how much it would mean to everyone involved, was overwhelming. It was a landmark moment that brought tears to the eyes of everyone who has been lucky enough to be a part of Jenny and British snowboarding's collective journey.

I said at the beginning that the hardship of British snowboarding nurtures modest and passionate talents who take nothing for granted. Jenny's win, and the way she celebrated it afterwards, proves the point. She was determined to share her glory with the scene that made her with the same grounded, self-deprecating humour that has always made British snowboarding so great.

And that is the lesson of British snowboarding. It isn't about how good you are. It's about friendship. Sure, riding with your friends means you'll push yourself. Sometimes that means slamming. Other times that means tapping into the euphoria of making a trick or doing something stylish in front of mates who are just as stoked as you are.

Above all, snowboarding lets you share the best and the worst times, and create bonds that in those moments can last a lifetime. British snowboarding is the proof, because if you've been a part of it at all during the last 30 years, you'll know it's like having a second family.

Ed Leigh is a British sports presenter, snowboarder, and commentator

Jenny Jones takes bronze at the Sochi 2014 Olympic Winter Games, Russia

THE ROAD TO PYEONGCHANG
BY MATT BARR

The birth of GB Park and Pipe as we know it today can be traced back to the same strong domestic roots outlined by Ed and Pat. As those chapters demonstrate, the UK's unique and thriving scene has long been legendary, thanks to an unquenchable stoke for skiing and snowboarding, and a diasporic culture that sees Brit seasonaires flock to Europe and North America's most progressive mountains each winter.

At the competitive level, the challenge was to shape this promising raw material into an organisational structure that could steer Britain's most promising talents to the top of the sport. It was a daunting prospect, requiring the establishment of a grassroots domestic pathway that took into account the unique conditions required to nurture freesports athletes, all packaged in a way that would unlock mainstream sports funding.

Efforts began in earnest during the 2007/2008 season, when British snowboarder, coach and scene stalwart Hamish McKnight was asked by Snowsport GB to develop a nascent freestyle team. Showing the clairvoyance that would become a hallmark of his coaching approach, McKnight's first move was to broaden the focus to include "our much larger potential strengths in slopestyle and big air, rather than halfpipe alone," a seemingly simple yet highly progressive insight that would ultimately lead to two Olympic medals within a decade.

For the next two years, Hamish worked with others to develop the foundational principles, and technical and reporting tools, that underpin the work of GB Park and Pipe to this day. In this, he was helped by snowboarder Lesley McKenna, at the time a volunteer advisor to Snowsport GB and somebody able to offer peerless advice and insights thanks to her experience as a pioneering Olympic competitor.

Others were also filling the gap with their own initiatives, notably Dan Wakeham, another Olympic alumnus who co-formed One Snowboarding, a precursor to what became the GB Junior Freestyle Snowboard Team. Meanwhile, around the same time and in the same ski areas, Pat Sharples was working with the ski athletes who would go on to become GB Park and Pipe team members, through aforementioned mechanisms such as the Grom Camps.

Two other individuals would become increasingly influential during these early years: Nelson Pratt and Jack Shackleton, as Hamish explains.

"Nelson was selected two years running as an athlete, and eventually coached alongside me. He really had an absolute passion that we could go on to do great things in the sport and showed complete belief in talents like Billy Morgan from the beginning. Jack's involvement in the early years of the team as an athlete alongside Nelson and then eventually as a coach who is still a key team member today was also crucial."

Another important development was Jenny Jones' increasing international success and profile, which definitively debunked the notion that a British athlete could never consistently challenge at the very top of the sport.

"Jenny's first X Games gold medal in 2009 really backed up our belief that the UK could help shape the future of slopestyle", explains Hamish. "At the time slopestyle wasn't an Olympic sport. But we knew that would change, and we needed to be ready when it did".

To that end, Hamish, Lesley and Pat began to develop the idea that would ultimately lead to the establishment of GB Park and Pipe as we know it today: a combined freeski and freestyle snowboarding team.

Billy Morgan lands the world-first BS quad cork 1800.
Mottolino Snowpark, Italy. 2015

Results at the time backed up this hunch, notably those clocked by skiers James Woods and Katie Summerhayes, who were already winning X Games slopestyle medals and FIS World Championships medals.

For Hamish, the key to this idea lay in the grassroots similarity between both disciplines.

"Of course, certain cultural rivalries remained. But combining freeskiing and snowboarding made sense at an organisational level and gave us the opportunity to take the entire project to the next level."

As long as the rest of the world caught up that is. Sure enough, in 2012, UK Sport officially decided to fund slopestyle development with National Lottery cash, vindicating Hamish's earlier insight. Soon after, British Ski and Snowboard officially asked Lesley, Pat and Hamish to put together a world class programme, and GB Park and Pipe as the entity we know today was born.

Official financial support from BSS and, eventually, outside sponsors, meant that future champions finally had the platform they needed to make the most of their prodigious natural talent and obvious potential.

Not that the coaches rested on their laurels. From the start, they concentrated on ensuring that the team's values - fun, passion, collaboration and progression - were authentic and credible. They also prioritised the needs of the athletes above everything else. "Our own experiences told us that empowering the athletes and putting them at the centre of the process would be key," says Lesley. "We also backed up what we knew personally with theoretical thinking from the cutting edge of performance coaching."

It was a unique approach that very quickly became globally respected. Some national teams, especially on the snowboarding side, had become notorious for running programmes in the more traditional summer training style, treating athletes as machines and alienating them in the process.

This was compounded by the long-standing enmity many freesports athletes felt towards the rigorous FIS-controlled system of Olympic qualification, something epitomised by Terje Haakonsen's notorious decision to boycott the inaugural Olympic snowboarding event at Nagano in 1998.

From the beginning, Lesley, Pat and Hamish were

Laax, Switzerland. 2017

determined to avoid the same trap by building a credible athlete-focussed ethos into the fabric of the entire GB Park and Pipe operation.

This spirit was not only projected within the team, but to the wider ski and snowboard community, which proved vital to the team's growing success and credibility both on and off the slope.

Their approach was vindicated within two years, when Jenny Jones won a ground-breaking bronze medal in slopestyle at the 2014 Sochi Olympics – Great Britain's first ever medal on snow. Behind the scenes, subsequent developments helped to consolidate this initial success and further justify the approach put in place by the coaching team – notably Katie Ormerod achieving a world-first backside double 1080 in May of that year.

The next key step was the introduction of Izzy Atkin to the squad from her family base in Park City, Utah. Her incredible natural ability had been immediately recognised by Pat. This was followed in 2015 by another world-first, Billy Morgan's now legendary backside 1800 quad cork. This pioneering achievement once more confirmed the prescience of McKnight's decision to focus on big air and slopestyle a decade earlier – something further underlined in 2015, when the IOC formally announced the inclusion of big air at the 2018 Games.

Yet this announcement in itself created new challenges for the coaches and riders. To qualify for each major competition, athletes must accumulate points towards their world ranking. This points system forms the basis of Olympic qualification, meaning that to qualify for PyeongChang GB athletes would need to ride as many big air contests as possible. These events often take place in front of huge crowds in challenging city environments, on big, steep jumps with bumpy drop-ins.

To help them prepare for this new challenge, the coaches decided to expose the athletes to as many of these unfamiliar contest environments as possible, something which paid dividends immediately when Katie Ormerod took World Cup gold during the big air event in Moscow at the beginning of 2017 – the first British woman to do so.

The environment of progression and innovation that the coaches had painstakingly nurtured was beginning to yield real results – and only months before the PyeongChang Olympics.

But Hamish McKnight, typically, was thinking bigger. For years, he'd been working on a plan to equip the team with their own giant airbag training facility, which would provide the team with a safe space to practise the type of tricks that could mean the difference between success and failure at the forthcoming Olympics.

As he explained at the time, "sport specific big airbag landings are an absolute game changer for our sports. They give athletes the opportunity to acquire and repeat tricks which carry an ever increasing and hugely impressive level of risk, and are basically a necessity for any elite athlete wishing to challenge the best in the world."

In December 2017, that long-held ambition became a reality as GB Park and Pipe partnered with Italian resort, Mottolino, to create an exclusive big airbag training facility.

It was the final part of a masterplan that had been ten years in the making. In that time, Britain's reputation on the global freeski and snowboarding stage had been completely transformed thanks to a run of results that included over 30 podium places, and a culture of progression and innovation epitomised by Billy Morgan's world first quad cork.

Above all, the coaches had pulled off something unique within the heavily controlled environment that is Olympic qualifying, by promoting a culture of complete self-expression and a skatepark mentality that enabled the athletes to perform at the highest possible level.

Just how successful this approach had been would become fully apparent at the 2018 Olympics.

Matt Barr is a journalist, director of All Conditions Media and runs the Looking Sideways action sports podcast.

Billy Morgan. BS 540 nose grab. Legs of Steel, Zurs, Austria. 2015

Woodsy. Truck driver 720. Cardrona, New Zealand. 2016

Katie Ormerod. Wins the Moscow Big Air. Russia. 2017

GB Park and Pipe Love Skiing / Love Snowboarding campaign. Perisher, Australia. 2016

Katie Summerhayes. 360 tail grab over the Nine Queens castle. Sunrise at Serfaus-Fiss-Ladis, Austria. 2016

Jack Shackleton. Laax, Switzerland. 2017

Hamish McKnight coaches Katie Ormerod. Laax, Switzerland. 2017

Katie Ormerod. Backflip. Laax Open, Switzerland. 2017

Aimee Fuller. Alley-oop andrecht. Perisher, Australia. 2016

Aimee Fuller. Laax, Switzerland. 2017

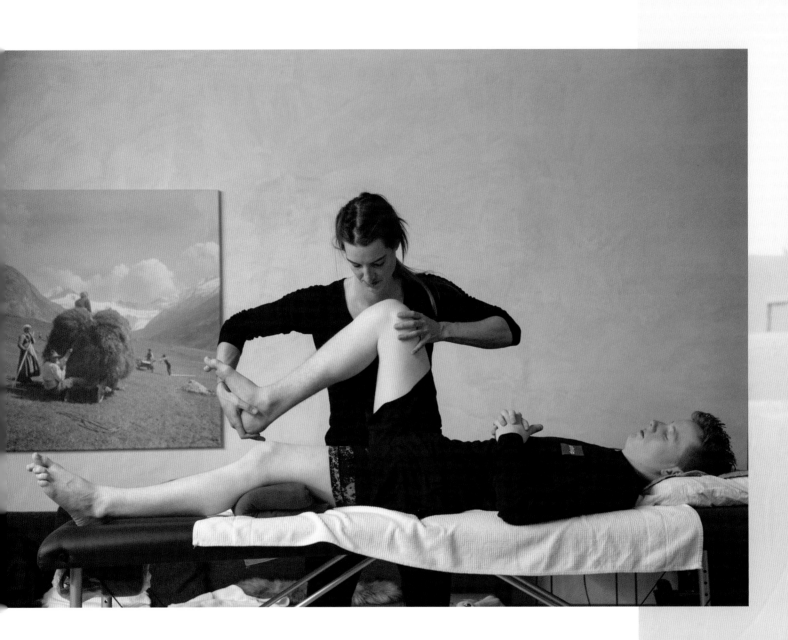

Following a tear in his medial meniscus, Matt McCormick undergoes
physiotherapy with Lisa Filzmoser. The Rocksresort, Laax. 2017

Still able to ride, Matt McCormick's front blunt 270 off.
Laax Open, Switzerland. 2017

Billy Morgan. Laax, Switzerland. 2017

Billy Morgan. BS 720 melon. Stoneham Mountain, Quebec, Canada. 2017

Jamie Nicholls. Perisher, Australia. 2016

Jamie Nicholls. Cab 1080. Snow Jamboree, Stoneham Mountain, Quebec, Canada. 2017

Cal Sandieson. Switch double 900. Snow Jamboree, Stoneham Mountain, Quebec, Canada. 2017

GB Park and Pipe in Quebec, Canada. 2017

Katie Ormerod. BS 720.
Snow Jamboree big air, Quebec City, Canada. 2017

Jamie Nicholls. Switch boardslide 270 out. Snow Jamboree slopestyle final, Stoneham Mountain, Quebec, Canada. 2017

Billy Morgan. Lake Silvaplana, Switzerland. 2017

Izzy Atkin. Lake Silvaplana, Switzerland. 2017

Billy Morgan. FS 360. The Stomping Ground Snowpark, Corvatsch 3303, Switzerland. 2017

Katie Ormerod. Lake Silvaplana, Switzerland. 2017

Katie Ormerod. Backflip. The Stomping Ground Snowpark, Corvatsch 3303, Switzerland. 2017

Woodsy. Double tail grab 720. Cardrona, New Zealand. 2016

Murray Buchan. Cardrona, New Zealand. 2016

Rowan Cheshire. Cardrona, New Zealand. 2016

Madi Rowlands. Lipslide 270 out. Perisher, Australia. 2016

Anna Vincenti. Perisher, Australia. 2016

Billy Morgan. Perisher, Australia. 2016

Mike Rowlands. Switch cork 7. Perisher, Australia. 2016

Billy Morgan. Miller flip. Perisher, Australia. 2016

Matt McCormick. Eurocarve. Corvatsch, Switzerland. 2017

Matt McCormick. Lake Silvaplana, Switzerland. 2017

Tyler Harding. Lake Silvaplana, Switzerland. 2017

Rowan Coultas. Michalchuk. The Stomping Ground Snowpark, Corvatsch 3303, Switzerland. 2017

Cal Sandieson. Handplant. The Stomping Ground Snowpark, Corvatsch 3303, Switzerland. 2017

Matt McCormick. BS 180 Japan. The Stomping Ground Snowpark,
Corvatsch 3303, Switzerland. 2017

Ongoing physio for Matt McCormick with Lisa Filzmoser. Lake
Silvaplana, Switzerland. 2017

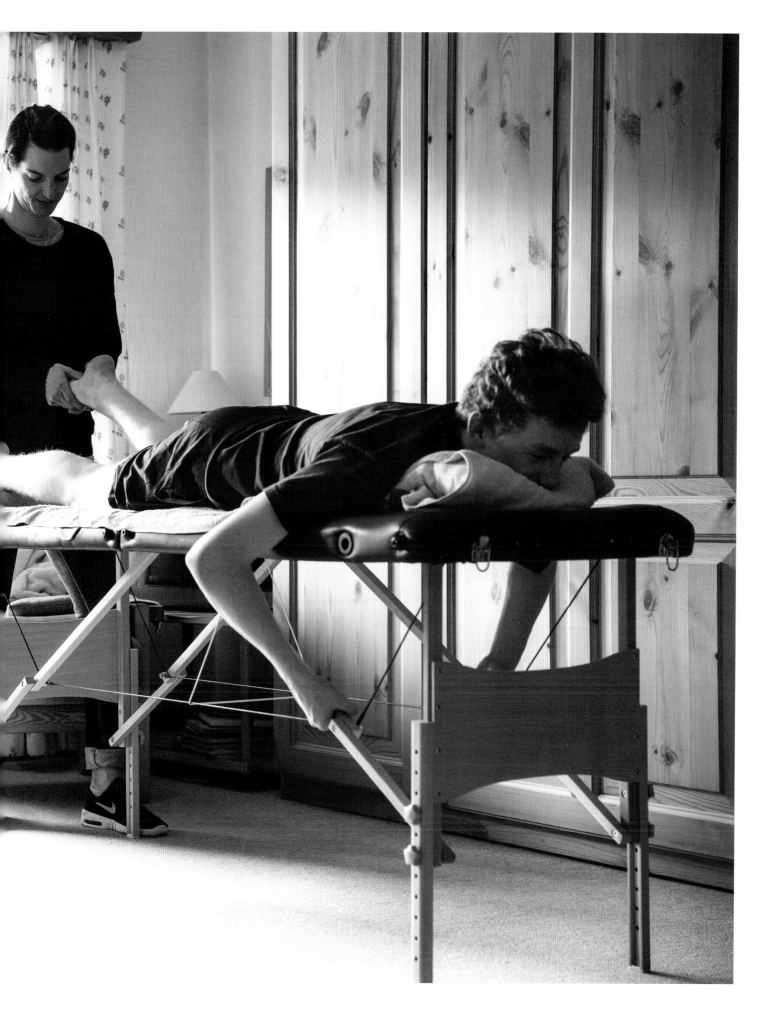

Acrobatics and Athletics Coach Ross Hill put's the team through their paces. Livigno, Italy. 2017

Aimee Fuller. Holland Park, London, England. 2017

Katie Summerhayes. Halifax Ski & Snowboard Centre, England. 2017

Tyler Harding. Right cork 720 blunt. Halifax Ski & Snowboard Centre, England. 2017

Jack Shackleton, BS disaster and Billy Morgan, FS smith.
Saughton Skatepark, Edinburgh, Scotland. 2017

Madi Rowlands. 540 mute.
Stubai Glacier, Austria. 2016

Katie Ormerod. BS 720.
Stubai Glacier, Austria. 2017

Mottolino Snowpark, Italy. 2017

Rowan Coultas. First hit. BigAirBag pre-Olympic
training. Mottolino Snowpark, Italy. 2017

Mike Rowlands, switch double 1080.
Mottolino Snowpark, Italy. 2017

Harris Booth, right double 1260 inside safety.
Mottolino Snowpark, Italy. 2017

Aimee Fuller. Cab double underflip.
Mottolino Snowpark, Italy. 2017

Katie Ormerod. Double backflip. Mottolino Snowpark, Italy. 2017

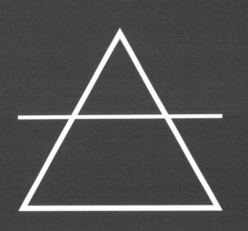

THE 2018 WINTER OLYMPICS
BY ED LEIGH

If Jenny Jones's slopestyle bronze at the 2014 Games in Sochi was an indication that the GB Park and Pipe team were on the right track, a couple of subsequent developments confirmed it in spectacular style.

The first was when 16-year-old Katie Ormerod became the first female snowboarder to land a double cork 1080. Then, the following year, Billy Morgan became the first snowboarder to land a quad cork, to global acclaim.

These incredible, world-first feats sent shockwaves through the snowboarding and skiing world, proving that the breakneck pace of progression that characterises elite level skiing and snowboarding would not be slowing down. And, as unlikely as it seemed, it would be British athletes leading the charge.

The 2015 announcement that Big Air would be included in the 2018 Games only added to the sense of anticipation. At that point, only two other athletes had managed to land the quad cork, while Katie was still out on her own as the only woman to stomp the double 10.

It was an incredibly exciting time for GB Park and Pipe, and as a close observer it was very difficult not to get carried away with the thought of more medals on the horizon. Still, as anybody with any knowledge of action sports knows, three years is a lifetime in elite freestyle skiing and snowboarding. Progression at all costs is like a plague that infects the most talented, dramatically dragging the sports forward with each passing winter.

The feats of athletes like Jenny, Woodsy, Billy and Katie proved that GB Park and Pipe was now at the forefront of this evolutionary charge, achieving world firsts in a sporting environment previously dominated by the North American and Scandinavian superpowers, and on the cusp of becoming a genuine snow sports powerhouse.

As we've seen, the behind-the-scenes work that had enabled this dramatic leap forward had been going on for the best part of a decade.

The decision made by Lesley McKenna, Pat Sharples and Hamish McKnight to combine the ski and snowboard teams into one entity and share all training and coaching facilities was at the time unheard of. Yet its success has seen almost every major nation adopt the same practice.

There is no doubt that all of these logistical and economic advantages played a role in speeding up development for GB Park and Pipe athletes. But to my mind, the most important breakthrough of all was a much less tangible, more holistic concept that truly gave the athletes the ideological platform to succeed. Lesley McKenna, who came up with the idea, calls it Radical Gains.

The concept of Radical Gains shows a sophisticated understanding of what makes action sports progression unique, and why attempting to train elite action sports athletes using traditional methods is doomed to failure.

It is based upon the idea that there are two ways of motivating people: extrinsic and intrinsic. Extrinsic basically means the carrot and the stick. Or, in this context, medals, money and fame versus obscurity and a lack of recognition.

Intrinsic motivation comes down to the idea of personal satisfaction, something that is integral to the principle of

The grounds of the Gyeonghoeru Palace overlooking Seoul, South Korea

progression in action sports. Put simply, it is the idea of doing something because you enjoy doing it and because it gives you a chance to learn and explore your own potential, rather than because you think you'll get something back.

This seemingly simple yet revolutionary concept, that elite action sports athletes will only fulfil their potential if they are enabled to motivate themselves intrinsically, underpinned Lesley, Hamish and Pat's entire coaching strategy and is to me what was fundamentally responsible for the team's spectacular subsequent success.

What I love about this philosophy more than anything else is that it makes medal-chasing a by-product of a successful coaching process, rather than an absolute means to an end.

Long term, it means the athlete experience is ultimately a liberating one, ensuring they are able to value themselves and their achievements way beyond the transient value of an Olympic medal. Like I say, sophisticated, revolutionary and uniquely action sports.

It was against this backdrop that the GB Park and Pipe team

Goseong Unification Observatory. Views into North Korea overlooking the Geumgangsan Mountains and the Korean Demilitarised Zone.

travelled to Korea as part of the biggest GB team ever taken to a Winter Games. James Woods, Jamie Nicholls, Katie Summerhayes, Izzy Atkin, Billy Morgan and Katie Ormerod all went in with high expectations, their form going into the Games suggesting they were all capable of winning medals. For the remaining teammates, it was an opportunity to gain valuable experience.

Did they succeed? By any traditional measure of sporting success, of course, as those two bronze medals for Billy and Izzy demonstrate.

But at a deeper level, the story of PyeongChang, and GB Park and Pipe as a whole, is about how a group of visionaries have created a sensitive sporting culture that has enabled a generation of action sports athletes to achieve – yes – radical gains and global mainstream sporting success in the unlikeliest possible way.

I can't wait to see where we go from here.

Olympic Village: Izzy Atkin, Alison Robb, Jamie Matthew, Murray
Buchan, Katie Summerhayes, Pat Sharples and Rowan Cheshire

North Korean cheerleaders at the PyeongChang 2018
Winter Olympic Games opening ceremony

Phoenix Snowpark

Team GB Wax Technician BJ Mazzola and GB Park and Pipe Assistant Snowboard Coach Jack Shackleton

Phoenix Snowpark

Murray Buchan. Switch 720 Japan. Men's ski halfpipe qualification

Billy Morgan. Cab triple underflip. Men's snowboard slopestyle qualification

Rowan Coultas. Cab 5. Men's snowboard slopestyle practice

Jamie Nicholls. FS 1080. Men's snowboard slopestyle qualification

Katie Ormerod. Women's snowboard slopestyle practice

Aimee Fuller. 50/50. Women's snowboard slopestyle final

Woodsy. Japan over hitching post. Men's freeski slopestyle

Tyler Harding. Right double cork 1260. Men's freeski slopestyle qualification

Woodsy. Left triple cork 1440. Men's freeski slopestyle final

Izzy Atkin. Rail slide on the hitching post. Women's freeski slopestyle qualification

Woodsy. Double cork 1260 blunt. Men's freeski slopestyle qualification

Katie Summerhayes. Rail slide. Women's freeski slopestyle qualification

Katie Summerhayes. Left 540 tail grab. Women's freeski slopestyle final

Izzy Atkin wins bronze at the women's Olympic freeski slopestyle at Phoenix Snowpark

Bronze medalist Izzy Atkin of Great Britain celebrates during the medal ceremony for the women's freeski slopestyle at the PyeongChang Olympic Plaza. Izzy is the first British skier to win an Olympic medal.

Woodsy. Left triple cork 1440. Men's freeski slopestyle

Alexander Glavatsky-Yeadon. Cork 7. Men's ski halfpipe qualification

Molly Summerhayes. Air to fakie. Women's ski halfpipe practice

Murray Buchan. Left 900 tail grab. Men's ski halfpipe qualification

Peter Speight. Cork 900. Men's ski halfpipe qualification

Rowan Cheshire and Pat Sharples following Rowan's 7th place finish

Lesley McKenna, Rowan Cheshire, Jamie Matthew, Alison Robb and Pat Sharples

Rowan Cheshire. Alley-oop mute. Women's ski halfpipe final

Alpensia, PyeongChang, South Korea

The debut Olympic big air. Alpensia Ski Jumping Stadium

Jamie Nicholls. Cab 1080. Men's snowboard big air qualification

Jamie Nicholls. Switch FS 1440. Men's snowboard big air qualification

Rowan Coultas. BS triple 1440. Men's snowboard big air qualification

Billy Morgan. Men's big air final test session

Billy Morgan. FS triple 1440. Men's snowboard big air practice

Billy Morgan. FS triple 1440 double grab.
Men's snowboard Olympic big air final

Billy Morgan. BS triple 1440 nose grab.
Men's snowboard Olympic big air final

Billy Morgan wins Olympic bronze at the men's snowboard big air

Celebrations as Billy Morgan wins bronze for Great Britain at the medal
ceremony for the snowboard big air. PyeongChang Olympic Plaza

The Gyeongbokgung Palace, Seoul

Admiral Yi Sun-Sin statue, Seoul

THE FUTURE
BY LESLEY MCKENNA

The future for the GB Park and Pipe team is really promising. We've worked hard to create a tangible pathway for British talent, meaning we can identify kids at Championship Ski and Snowboard league level, then track their progress through the ranks via the international world of park and pipe snowboarding and national contests like the Brits.

This framework means we have a hugely talented crew of young skiers and snowboarders coming through. Snowboarders like Mia Brookes and Gabe Adams represent a bright future, and they're already at the top of their age groups in contests like the Rookie Tour. We also have ski athletes like Kirsty Muir and Zoe Atkins at the top of their age groups in ski slopestyle and ski halfpipe, too.

Even more promisingly, these youngsters have grown up with the current crop of GB Park and Pipe athletes as role models. They know it is possible to achieve first tricks themselves - because they've already seen UK snow athletes achieve that very thing.

Those senior role models include skiers and snowboarders at the top level who still have long careers in front of them. Athletes like Katie Ormerod, Katie Summerhayes, Izzy Atkin, James Woods, Jamie Nicholls and Rowan Cheshire have all achieved World Cup podium places already. Of course Izzy took bronze in the 2018 Olympics, and they will all be aiming for the 2022 Games.

Then we have athletes like Rowan Coultas, Matt McCormick, Madi Rowlands and Tyler Harding breaking through, each of whom are about to make the next step and achieve podium level.

The challenge for the GB Park and Pipe team is to keep doing things differently in a way that supports our athletes' unique backgrounds and skill sets.

Our goal is still to keep our values of fun, passion, progression and collaboration at the forefront, meaning that learning new tricks with your friends will continue to be at the heart of what we do on a day-to-day basis - even when they are the hardest tricks in the world.

To maintain our edge, we will need to be flexible enough to spot the challenges ahead before they are upon us, ensuring we can solve each one in the most practical and efficient way possible. We also need to keep the athletes themselves at the centre of the process. In high performance sport, this is easier said than done, but we think that the unique culture and community we have around us here in the UK will help keep us on the right path.

The world of human performance is a very exciting place to be working right now, and action sports is at the forefront. Being able to support the conditions needed to help the athletes make the leap of faith required to land a world first trick, for example, is an area in science that is currently getting a lot of attention, and something that is at the centre of our coaching process.

The feeling you get when you land a trick, whether your first 360 or the world's first quad cork, is integral to all

Pathway athletes Sam Gaskin and Billy Cockrell compete during
the Brits ski and snowboard championship. Laax, Switzerland. 2018

Euan Baxter, Performance Coach for Snowsports Scotland, with Roahan Duncan. The Brits, Laax, Switzerland. 2018

action sports progression. In a coaching context, we call it the Radical Gains moment, with the feeling engendered by your new level of progression the stoke that every skier, snowboarder, surfer or skateboarder knows all too well.

We believe that as long as we can continue to support our athletes as they aim for their own individual radical gains, we're heading in the right direction. If we can also support the athletes by way of current technology and thinking in all other areas of human performance, then GB Park and Pipe can remain at the forefront of the freestyle ski and snowboard world for years to come.

Part of the picture when it comes to supporting stoke in the way that we aim to, is that the athletes must really love what they are doing.

Just to be able to ski and snowboard in the UK takes a certain level of perseverance and dedication, which in turn develops a high level of passion for the sports. We do think that this gives us a bit of an advantage over the other teams, or at least makes up for some of our inherent disadvantages.

As long as passion is high and the stoke is there, we can keep the radical gains coming and keep mixing it at the top.

Lesley McKenna is Programme Manager for GB Park and Pipe

Peter Speight with Pat Sharples. Laax, Switzerland. 2018

Peter Speight. Flare mute. The Brits freeski halfpipe final.
Laax, Switzerland. 2018

Alexander Glavatsky-Yeadon. Corked 9 satans seatbelt.
Freeski halfpipe winner. The Brits, Laax, Switzerland. 2018

Jamie Nicholls. Laax, Switzerland. 2018

Rowan Coultas. Layback. Laax, Switzerland. 2018

Rowan Coultas. Laax, Switzerland. 2018

Neil MacGrain with Ben and Hannah Kinnear. British Ski and Snowboard Lecht Winter Games. Lecht, Scotland. 2018

Photography

Nick Atkins: 25, 26, 29, 30, 183

Ilanna Barkusky: 44-45

Matt Georges: 42-43, 48, 56, 78-85

Jamie Johnston, 22

Emma Kennedy: 167

Pally Learmond: 10, 13, 38-39, 102, 103

Jamie Matthew: 120

Natalie Mayer: 21, 22, 184

Neil MacGrain: 10

Steven McKenna: 2-3, 180-181

James McPhail: 20

Red Bull Media: 34-35

Sam Mellish: 27, 36, 46, 47, 49, 50-55, 57-71, 86-101, 104-113, 116-120, 120-167, 167-169, 172-179

Dan Milner: 16-17, 23

Joe Morgan: 31

James North: 22

Camilla Rutherford: 9

Tommy Pyatt: 40, 72-77

Russ Shea: 11, 22, 183

Melody Sky: 8, 13

David Spurdens: 18, 19

Kirill Umrikhin: 41

Mike Weyerhaeuser/JDP: 14, 15, 24, 25, 28, 30

Ross Woodhall: 6-7, 12

Cover photo: Billy Morgan at the PyeongChang Olympic big air final, South Korea by Sam Mellish

RADICAL GAINS: THE GB PARK AND PIPE STORY

Copyright © diesel books, 2018. All rights reserved
First published in the United Kingdom in 2018 by diesel books.

ISBN: 978-0-9566928-4-9
First Edition - Limited to 500
Printed and bound by Biddles, Kings Lynn, Great Britain.

A CIP catalogue record for this book is available from the British Library.

Introduced by Ed Leigh and Pat Sharples
Contributions from Matt Barr, Lesley McKenna and Hamish McKnight
Edited by Sam Mellish
Editorial supervision and copy editing by Matt Barr and Harry Mitchell Thompson
Art direction by diesel books
Design by diesel books and Andy McGarity
Images © named photographer

To see more from diesel books, please go to:
www.dieselbooks.co.uk

You can make contact with us here: info@dieselbooks.co.uk

Acknowledgments

diesel books would like to thank the following, without whose contributions this book would not have been possible. We would also like to thank Lesley McKenna, Pat Sharples, Hamish McKnight, Harry Mitchell Thompson, Ed Leigh and Matt Barr for their ongoing support as well as GB Park and Pipe for allowing this project to organically develop and grow.

Jim Adlington, Colin Andrews, TSA - The Snowboard Asylum, Izzy Atkin, Nick Atkins, Ilanna Barkusky, Matt Barr, Euan Baxter, The BigAirBag, Ed Blomfield, Harris Booth, Fin Bremner, BSS, Murray Buchan, Rowan Cheshire, Rowan Coultas, Lisa Filzmoser, Aimee Fuller, Team GB, Nathan Gallagher, Matt Georges, Alexander Glavatsky-Yeadon, Tyler Harding, Dom Harrington, Ross Hill, UK Snowboard History, Colin Holden, Richard Husseiny, Mike Weyerhaeuser/JDP, Jamie Johnston, Jenny Jones, Susi Jursik, Emma Kennedy, Tristan Kennedy, Ben Kilner, Ben Kinnear, Pally Learmond, Ed Leigh, Emma Longsdale, UK Lottery Funding, James Machon, Kat MacKenzie, Jamie Matthew, Natalie Mayer, BJ Mazzola, Chris McCormick, Matt McCormick, Neil MacGrain, Lesley McKenna, Steven McKenna, Alex McKeown, Hamish McKnight, Josie McNamara, James McPhail, Red Bull Media, Pat Meurier, Dan Milner, Brett Moore, Billy Morgan, Joe Morgan, Sophie Morrison, Paddy Mortimer, Jon Moy, Adrain Myres, Jamie Nicholls, James North, Katie Ormerod, Tommy Pyatt, Alison Robb, Madi Rowlands, Mike Rowlands, Cal Sandieson, Henry Shackleton, Jack Shackleton, Pat Sharples, UK Sport, Russ Shea, Melody Sky, Jeremy Sladen, Peter Speight, David Spurdens, Camilla Rutherford, Katie Summerhayes, Molly Summerhayes, Dave Tallon, Joe Tyler, Kirill Umrikhin, Anna Vincenti, Katrina Vines, Dan Wakeham, Ross Woodhall and James Woods.

The GB Park and Pipe Team programme is UKSport Lottery funded.

Follow @GBparkandpipe for the latest news.

Founders of GB Park and Pipe:
Lesley McKenna, Pat Sharples and Hamish McKnight.

Nelson in Devon, May 2012

Ride On